26 New Etudes

for

TRUMPET

in

13 major and 13 minor keys

with scales & arpeggios

- for advanced players -

Robert J. Brownlow

26 New Etudes for Trumpet: In 13 major and 13 minor keys with scales & arpeggios

Author/Composer: Robert J. Brownlow

Copyright © 2015 **Robert J. Brownlow**
Copyright © 2015 **Back To Classic Music In Print Ltd**.

Akron, Ohio

All rights reserved. Any type of reproduction and distribution of this book as a whole or any part of the whole, in paper or any digital/electronic formats, for personal, professional, and commercial purposes are prohibited without permission. Storing in any electronic database, web/cloud, other digital means, and data retrieval systems without proper authorization are also prohibited.

For inquiries email: *info@back2classic.us*

Prepared for publication: by V.V. Brownlow

Library of Congress Control Number: 2016948867

ISBN-10: 0692439994
ISBN-13: 978-0692439999

Printed-On-Demand

[this page is left intentionally blank]

PREFACE

It is important that aspiring musicians become fluent in all of the major and minor keys. When I was a student, I was never entirely satisfied with the few choices of resources that contained well-written etudes in all keys.

There have been some attempts but many of them have some standard keys missing, others are purely technical and lacking in musicality. Others were too high or too long and left them out of reach of emerging players. Further, finding a single resource that laid out all of the major and minor scales and arpeggios in a simpler manner was more difficult than it should have been.

I did not need or want several pages of the same scale written out in a dozen or more rhythmic patterns and meters. As a result, I started playing the scales from memory in a manner that suited me. I have included these scales in this book. I also wrote them in such a way to include arpeggios at the end of each scale. This eliminates the need to have separate scales and arpeggio exercises.

I recommend that all players from emerging ones to professionals play all the major and minor scales every day. Once the scales are memorized, the player will be ready to begin playing them with more speed. Eventually, all the scales can be played quite quickly and be completed in a very short time. At this point, you will find that many things may be easier for you as a player: sight-reading, transposition, or improvisation for example.

THE ETUDES

I have attempted to write etudes that are accessible enough for young, emerging players but still be enjoyable and challenging by even the most advanced players. I tried to avoid writing in a purely technical manner and made a concerted effort to make them musically rewarding, fun to play, and diverse in style and material.

Of the 26 etudes, 24 of them are in a unique time signature. Only 4/4 and 6/8 time were used twice. While a few of the meters I chose are rarely used in common practice, it is still important that students are familiar with them. Too many etude books write in only a handful of the most common time signatures and as a result, the rhythmic patterns in the etudes tend to fall in similar and predictable patterns.

I made a conscious effort to keep the length of every etude manageable. Some etudes are too long for younger players and they become tests of endurance rather than of technique and musicality. Along these same lines, I avoided writing notes above concert G5. This way, most of these etudes will be able to be played even by players whose range is still developing. These are not meant to be range building exercises. That can be addressed in other books, methods and in consultation with your teacher.

In the etudes and scales in this book, I chose to favor the 5 flat/sharp keys over their 7 sharp/flat enharmonically equivalent keys. This seemed justified since the fingerings are the same for: B major and C-flat major, D-flat and C# major, b-flat and a# minor and g# and a-flat minor. Further, the chances of needing to play music in keys with 7 flats or sharps are very small, especially when one has an option of choosing trumpets pitched in keys other than b-flat concert.

TEMPO MARKINGS

I did place a metronome marking at the beginning of every etude. They are merely suggestions. Some of them may need to be played slower, especially at first. Others you may choose to play faster than the suggested.

ARTICULATIONS AND BREATH MARKS

Selecting articulations for passages is not an exact science. During the editing process I changed many of them from my original marking as I played through them. You should feel free to adjust the articulations and even to experiment with them to suit your needs and desires. Or, you may leave them just as they are. The same goes for the suggested breath marks.

ON THE MINOR SCALES

There is a dilemma when practicing minor scales. Should you play melodic minor, harmonic, natural, a combination of two or all three of them? Further, when playing scales in one octave it is not possible to play all three versions of the minor scale unless you play each scale more than once. That is certainly an option, as is playing natural minor one day, harmonic another, melodic on the third day, and then every fourth day start the cycle again. I have provided some solutions to this problem.

OTHER BENEFITS

Having been a teacher of music theory for a number of years, I cannot stress enough the importance and benefits of knowing all major and minor scales and arpeggios. The reasons for this are too numerous to explain here. What I can say is that having scales memorized, and being able to recall them quickly will help with the study of intervals, triads, aids melodic dictation skills and more. All of the aforementioned topics are an integral part of any higher education music theory course.

~ Robert J. Brownlow

Key Signatures

Major key signatures:

	G	D	A	E	B	F#	C#
C							
	F	B♭	E♭	A♭	D♭	G♭	C♭

Minor key signatures:

	e	b	f#	c#	g#	d#	a#
a							
	d	g	c	f	b♭	e♭	a♭

Capital letter = Major key sign. Lower case letter = minor key sign. Arabic numbers refer to how many sharps or flats each key signature has.

Circle of Fifths

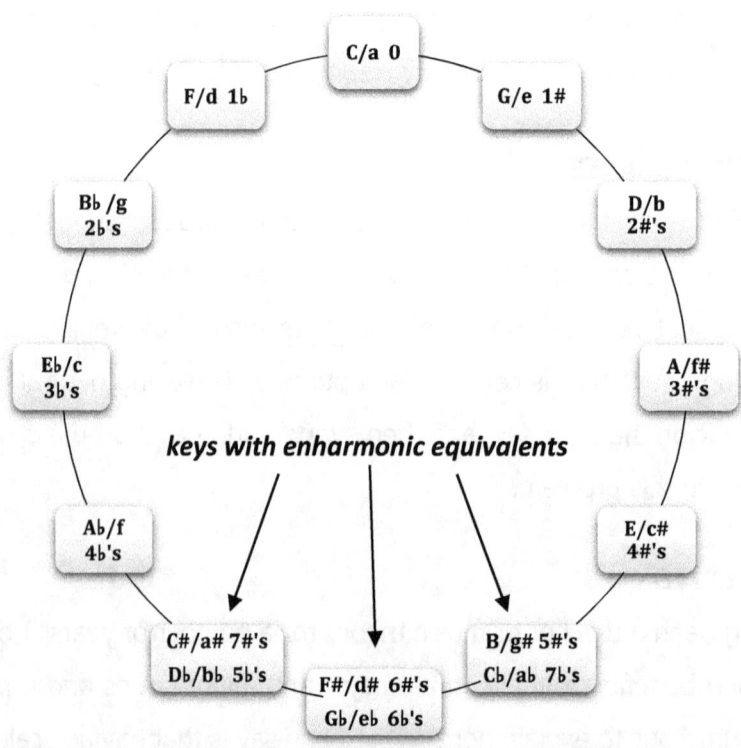

As you proceed clockwise around the circle, you add one sharp at each step. Going counter-clockwise you add 1 flat. All keys with 5 or more sharps and flats have an enharmonically equivalent key sign (see C♭ and B for example) which allows for the avoidance of keys using seven sharps or flats if desired.

Explanation of time signatures

Simple meter can be defined as: grouping of rhythms in which the beat is subdivided into two. The top number is most often a 2, 3, or 4. The bottom number indicates how many beats there are in one measure.

Simple meters utilized in these etudes are:

$\frac{2}{8}$ $\frac{3}{8}$ $\frac{4}{8}$ $\frac{2}{4}$ $\frac{3}{4}$ $\frac{4}{4}$ $\frac{2}{2}$ $\frac{3}{2}$ $\frac{4}{2}$

Compound meter can be defined as: groupings of rhythms in which the beat divides into groups of 3 rather than 2, and the unit of beat is always a dotted note.

Compound meters utilized in these etudes are:

$\frac{6}{8}$ $\frac{9}{8}$ $\frac{12}{8}$ $\frac{15}{8}$ $\frac{6}{4}$ $\frac{12}{4}$ $\frac{6}{16}$ $\frac{12}{16}$ $\frac{18}{16}$

Asymmetrical meter can be defined as: groupings where the top number is odd and therefore cannot be divided into equal beats.

Asymmetrical meters utilized in these etudes are:

$\frac{5}{8}$ $\frac{7}{8}$ $\frac{11}{8}$ $\frac{5}{4}$ $\frac{7}{4}$ $\frac{5}{2}$

Order of *Etudes*

The etudes are presented in the following pattern that follows the circle of fifths and adds one sharp or flat in each successive etude:

    C Major
    a minor
        G Major
        e minor
            F Major
            d minor
                D Major
                b minor
                    B♭ Major
                    g minor
                        A Major
                        f♯ minor
                            E♭ Major
                            c minor
                        E Major
                        c♯ minor
                    A♭ Major
                    f minor
                B Major
                g♯ minor
            D♭ Major
            b♭ minor
        F♯ Major
        d♯ minor
    G♭ Major
    e♭ minor

C Major

Robert J. Brownlow

a minor

Robert J. Brownlow

G Major

Robert J. Brownlow

This etude can be played much faster if the player can double tongue.

Robert J. Brownlow

e minor

Robert J. Brownlow

F Major

d minor

Robert J. Brownlow

Robert J. Brownlow

D Major

b minor

Robert J. Brownlow

Robert J. Brownlow

B♭ Major

Robert J. Brownlow

g minor

Robert J. Brownlow

A Major

Robert J. Brownlow

f# minor

This etude is based on a harmonic progression that was common during the renaissance era referred to as the *Passamezzo Antico*.

Back To Classic Music In Print Ltd.

12

E♭ Major

Robert J. Brownlow

Robert J. Brownlow

c minor

This etude requires the use of double tongue technique.

Robert J. Brownlow

E Major

c# minor

Robert J. Brownlow

If you have not yet learned to double tongue, play this etude at a fast single tougue speed. If you have learned to double tongue, feel free to play this as fast as you can.

Robert J. Brownlow

A♭ Major

Robert J. Brownlow

f minor

Robert J. Brownlow

B Major

Robert J. Brownlow

g# minor

Robert J. Brownlow

D♭ Major

Robert J. Brownlow

b♭ minor

Robert J. Brownlow

F# Major

d# minor

Robert J. Brownlow

Robert J. Brownlow

e♭ minor

[this page is left intentionally blank]

Robert J. Brownlow

Order of *Scales & Arpeggios*

Major and minor scales and arpeggios in all keys.

MAJOR

1 octave, ascending/descending, flat keys
1 octave, ascending/descending, sharp keys
1 octave, descending/ascending, flat keys
1 octave, descending/ascending, sharp keys
1 octave, ascending/descending pattern, complete circle of fifths with accidentals.
1 octave, descending/ascending pattern, complete circle of fifths with accidentals.
1 octave, ascending/descending pattern, complete circle of fifths with accidentals, variant.
1 octave, descending/ascending pattern, complete circle of fifths with accidentals, variant.
2 octave, ascending/descending pattern, complete circle of fifths.

MINOR

1 octave, natural minor, ascending/descending pattern, sharp keys.
1 octave, natural minor, ascending/descending pattern, flat keys.
1 octave, natural minor, descending/ascending pattern, sharp keys.
1 octave, natural minor, descending/ascending pattern, flat keys.
1 octave, natural minor, complete circle of fifths with accidentals.

1 octave, harmonic minor, ascending/descending pattern, sharp keys.
1 octave, harmonic minor, ascending/descending pattern, flat keys.
1 octave, harmonic minor, descending/ascending pattern, sharp keys.
1 octave, harmonic minor, descending/ascending pattern, flat keys.
1 octave, harmonic minor, complete circle of fifths with accidentals.

1 octave, melodic minor, ascending/descending pattern, sharp keys.
1 octave, melodic minor, ascending/decsending pattern, flat keys.
1 octave, melodic minor, descending/ascending pattern, sharp keys.
1 octave, melodic minor, descending/ascending pattern, flat keys.
1 octave, melodic minor, complete circle of fifths with accidentals.
2 octave key of A natural, harmonic and melodic minor.
2 octave ascending/descending, melodic ascending, natural and harmonic descending.

Scales and Arpeggios

Robert J. Brownlow

Major scales and arpeggios, one octave, ascending-descending pattern. Through the circle of fifths, flat keys.

Major scales and arpeggios, one octave, ascending-descending pattern. Through the circle of fifths, sharp keys.

Robert J. Brownlow

Major scales and arpeggios, one octave, descending-ascending pattern, sharp keys.

Major scales and arpeggios, one octave, descending-ascending pattern, flat keys.

Back To Classic Music In Print Ltd.

30

Robert J. Brownlow

Major scales and arpeggios, one octave, ascending-descending pattern using accidentals (no key sign). Through the complete descending circle of fifths.

Robert J. Brownlow

Major scales and arpeggios, one octave, descending-ascending pattern using accidentals (no key sign). Through the complete descending circle of fifths.

(Enharmonically equivalent to C# Major)

(Enharmonically equivalent to G♭ Major)

(Enharmonic equivalent to C♭ Major)

Back To Classic Music In Print Ltd.

32

Robert J. Brownlow

Major scales and arpeggios variant version, one octave, ascending-descending pattern using accidentals (no key sign). Through the complete descending circle of fifths.

(Enharmonic equivalent to C♭ Major)

Robert J. Brownlow

Major scales and arpeggios variant version, one octave, descending-ascending pattern using accidentals (no key sign). Through the complete descending circle of fifths.

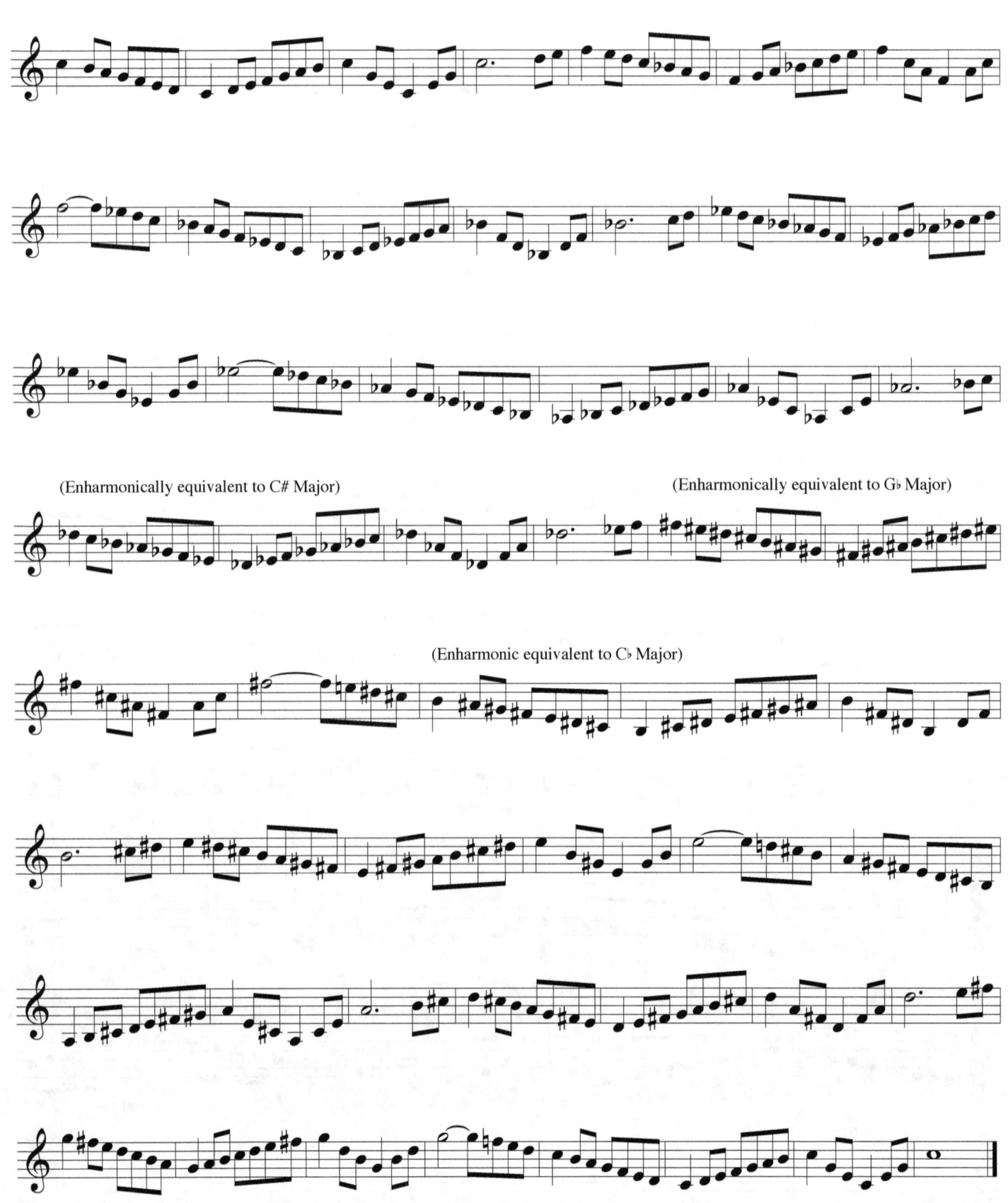

Robert J. Brownlow

Note: The descending/ascending pattern is not shown here. It could be done, although starting above C6 would be difficult for all but the strongest players.

Robert J. Brownlow

Minor scales and arpeggios, one octave, ascending-descending pattern, NATURAL minor. Circle of fifths through the sharp keys.

Minor scales and arpeggios, one octave, ascending-descending pattern, NATURAL minor. Circle of fifths through the flat keys.

Robert J. Brownlow

Minor scales and arpeggios, one octave, descending-ascending pattern, NATURAL minor. Circle of fifths through the sharp keys.

Minor scales and arpeggios, one octave, descending-ascending pattern, NATURAL minor. Circle of fifths through the flat keys.

Robert J. Brownlow

Minor scales and arpeggios, one octave, ascending/descending pattern, NATURAL minor. Complete circle of fifths, with accidentals.

Back To Classic Music In Print Ltd.

Robert J. Brownlow

Minor scales and arpeggios, one octave, ascending-descending pattern, HARMONIC minor. Circle of fifths through the sharp keys.

Minor scales and arpeggios, one octave, ascending-descending pattern, HARMONIC minor. Circle of fifths through the flat keys.

Robert J. Brownlow

Minor scales and arpeggios, one octave, descending-ascending pattern, HARMONIC minor. Circle of fifths through the sharp keys.

Back To Classic Music In Print Ltd.

Robert J. Brownlow

Minor scales and arpeggios, one octave, descending-ascending pattern, HARMONIC minor. Circle of fifths through the flat keys.

Minor scales and arpeggios, one octave, ascending/descending pattern, HARMONIC minor. Complete circle of fifths, with accidentals.

Back To Classic Music In Print Ltd.

42

Robert J. Brownlow

Minor scales and arpeggios, one octave, ascending-descending pattern, MELODIC minor variant. Circle of fifths through the sharp keys.

Minor scales and arpeggios, one octave, ascending-descending pattern, MELODIC minor variant. Circle of fifths through the flat keys.

Minor scales and arpeggios, one octave, descending/ascending pattern, MELODIC minor, circle of fifths through the sharp keys.

Robert J. Brownlow

Minor scales and arpeggios, one octave, descending/ascending pattern, MELODIC minor, circle of fifths through the flat keys.

Back To Classic Music In Print Ltd.

Robert J. Brownlow

Minor scales and arpeggios, one ocatve, ascending/descending pattern, MELODIC, complete circle of fifths with accidentals.

Back To Classic Music In Print Ltd.

46

Robert J. Brownlow

Playing two octave minor scales is more complex. You'll have to decide which form of the scales to play in which octave and so on. For starters, you could simply play all three version through the circle of fifths in their pure form as shown below.

NATURAL

HARMONIC

MELODIC

Playing all three forms of the minor scale in 2 octaves may be more than you feel is necessary. One solution to this problem is shown below. Here I have written out the pattern so that you'll play melodic minor when ascending and through the first octave descending (which coincides with natural minor) and harmonic in the 2nd octave descending. Other patterns are possible.
Make up one that suits your own needs.

Back To Classic Music In Print Ltd.

Robert J. Brownlow

[this page is left intentionally blank]

www.ingramcontent.com/pod-product-compliance
Lightning Source LLC
Chambersburg PA
CBHW060530010526
44110CB00052B/2558